unpack my heart with words

poems

Maureen Grady

2015

cover painting "Aura" by Aidan Ajándék

book design by Baz Here
author photo by Jane Olson

ISBN: 978-1514367087

Library of Congress Control Number: 1-2137038771

Printed in the United States of America

unpack my heart with words

Hamlet II.ii.

for Bronwyn and Aidan

CONTENTS

I Concave

i

ii

II Convex

I

Concave

i

Irish Grammar

In Irish,
we say that a feeling
is with, at, or upon us.
Sorrow is with me.
Anger is at me.
Love is upon me.
We do not have a feeling;
it has us.

Banshee

My child self hears no more cries from the crib,
just from Mommy, from Daddy.
Tonight the banshee wails too,
outside our windows,
circles the house howling.

I fear my newborn brother
will go with her.
They say he goes to God
and angels take him,
but I fear the banshee.

Her keening must wake the other babies
lost in the nether world,
longing for parents,
for earth,
for time.

I think I see his tiny hand
tangled in the vines and branches.
He cannot hear me when I say
Matthew, Matthew.

That night,
the banshee takes him away from us,
and as she leaves,
blows out the row of candles
burning at Mary's altar.

The Father's Tie

When my father was eight,
he stood at the deathbed of his father.
This dying man had studied to be a priest,
but fell in love instead.
He'd married a small and simple woman
of strength, humor, fire, and fathered five.
And though they did not have enough themselves,
he took food to families poorer than his own.
He worked, struggled, sickened, weakened,
and died too young.

My eight-year-old father stood and listened
for his father's final breath,
watched the thin chest rise and fall,
rise and fall, then rise no more.
The boy stood silent and said his last goodbye.
His prayers ushered the noble soul to rest.
This man knew God, was unafraid.
He'd given the boy the seed of life.

Later that night,
the boy who would become my father,
went to the closet where few clothes hung,
meager vestments for a life short-lived,
took out his father's only tie,
and tied it round his shirt collar.

Then he gathered his sisters, his brother,
his mother mad with grief,
around him and there, in that instant,
and forever after amen,
became the father.

First Love

That summer,
in California,
we swam daily
in my best friend's pool,
played like children-
mermaid, merman-
yet not quite children anymore.

I'd watch him dive into the pool
again and again,
athlete, clown, swain, boy, man,
her fatally beautiful cousin
from New York.

His smile, his bronzed body,
his wit, his great heart,
I was pierced through.

Those endless days
of heat and water,
eucalyptus and bougainvillea,
he shone his light upon me,
like a god.

I was too young then,
but awakened in his gaze.

That winter,
in New York,
he was gone.
A storm, an icy road,
the passenger seat,
a fatal skid,
sudden death.

There on the edge of that winter road,
the golden fire extinguished.
There on the edge of his radiant future.

A White Death

"Could they all wear white?" her mother asked.
All the children who loved her would be wearing white.
"And could they sing?" she asked.
"Could they all enter the church singing?"
The next day we would bury my best friend.

The day she died, the summer of our twelfth year,
we spoke seven times by phone.
I remember counting 7,
always my favorite number.
We had planned to spend that day,
all summer, our lives, together.

Each hour or so, we sent our voices over wire.
I remember words about my lost cat,
frustration with our mothers
unable to drive us to each other,
her newly-purchased dress, the heat.
Those seven conversations rise up
and stand before me, blind monoliths,
seven sphinxes I cannot get beyond.

I still seek each pearl and puzzle of that last day.
I reach back to see when death began,
imagine I hear her breath grow faint,
her true blue heart begin to fail.

We laughed until we cried that day,
not knowing death was listening on the line.

Fugue for the Fourth of July

On the summer day we buried her,
I went back to the house after the funeral.
Her mother took my hand,
drew me alone inside her room,
took out a new and patterned dress
with colors of the flag,
and handed it to me.
It was the dress her daughter
bought the day she died,
to celebrate a holiday
she would not live to live.

It was old-fashioned, patriotic, pure,
something from a book we would have loved,
the tag still strangely hanging from the sleeve.

Later, I hung it in my closet,
felt it silent there,
breathing in the dark,
a shade of her.

I wore it only once,
in the haven of my room,
one year later on the day she died.
I stood before the mirror trying to be her.
Although it fit, we had always worn each other's clothes,
it was not right.
It did not cover her lithe limbs,
the sweet bird-like neck, the blue-white skin,
her slowly failing heart.

So I hung it up again,
behind the many costumes of my life,
I took a small beloved pin she'd given me,
a golden cat with emerald eyes,
and fixed it at the heart place of the dress,
binding myself to her.

High School

Later that night,
he parked his proud car
down the street from my house,
saying it's early, smiling the smile.
I wondered was he confused,
with eyes closed he could find my house,
those many months spent circling me,
basting me before the flame.

And as his finger pushed the automatic door lock,
what I felt was love for him turned instantly to hate.
Gruff godless hands pull poke prod push
and diminish me to ash.
Just as a man goes to a verdant untouched land,
raises his foreign flag, and says,
this is mine.

We must be careful not to misname love.
I knew what every golden cell of me cried out for;
this was not it. He could not claim me.
I fought to release the lock.
No, I said. No. And ran toward home.

Lover

His skin is a river
that carries me.

The air howls around us,
and we are its echoes.

The lost light shapes us,
and we are wreathed by it.

His beauty blinds me to all,
but touch.

Sleep, Husband

It is the middle of the night,
and all around him
the shock of certain clouds.
I do not wake him.
He is perfect moon,
and blue-black hair breathing in this light.
A finely carved Athenian boy,
a summer peach of pleasure.
And I am his handmaiden
bringing limes and laurels,
summoning the pale blossoms.

He has come to this place to lie with me,
ten years now of waking next to him.
Our marriage is a golden spoon,
and we live in a rounded hour.
Our two young children,
bright constellations,
burn in the next room,
heavy with dream and wings.
Have I not told him
each day I loved him?
Each clock face stares,
saying what I fear most,
that he could die before me.

I give him all my threads to follow,
not to miss one green leaf of life,
one stone we are carving.

La Petite Mort

In sex
we learn
to be two
to be one
to be born
to live
to die
to come back to life.

The Face

My sleeping daughter's face
is such a flower I have never seen.
The brows, chiseled half-moons,
opal lids, a blue web of veins, sheer as silk.
Each lash, a small bird's wing.
The nose, two ink marks on new paper,
her hair adrift, flung mermaid-like,
one damp strand of kelp awash her neck.
An ear just visible, a silent shell,
and cheeks flushed with heat and dream.
Her lips pursed, asking something I cannot know.
The breath, a cloud of her life issuing forth,
and such a chin, the Sculptor's finest hour,
the fine angles etched in gold.

All is gilded,
yes, gilded all.

Boy from Budapest

When at rest
he curls against me,
half-bear, half-boy,
a pure roundness,

it is as if
my belly's moon
had grown with him,
each day, each hour,
forty weeks of wonder.

As if
I'd made him,
blood, bone, sinew, teeth,
each golden strand of hair.

As if
I'd pushed him
into the waiting world,
poured him from my loins,
into life.

No, it is more than this.
It is that he came to me,
as love comes,
and we know it to be love,
as morning comes,
and we awaken.

Painting the Room After Adopting Our Boy

Dark, dark he cries delightedly,
spinning till he falls in glee,
in two-year-old rapture.
His newly emerald room,
his gilded sapphire sky.

He yanks the velvet curtains closed,
first burgundy, then plum.
Then opens them again.
It's magic, he decides,
with day shut out.

This deep Venetian chamber,
a rich jeweled box,
closes round him,
more fitting for the man he will become.
And there he stands, a small sun god.

Later, as he sleeps,
besotted by images of moon,
his dreaming head shines in this den of night,
his spun gold strands of hair, sacred fibers,
filaments of light.

more fitting for the man
he will become.
And there he stands,
a small sun god.

his dreaming head shines
in this den of night,
his spun gold strands of hair,
sacred fibers,
filaments of light.

The world cannot be dark
now that he is safely here.

SFO to LAX

I'm afraid to fly today.
The nurses sitting across the aisle from me are looking to get laid,
off for a wild weekend in Little Rock, they say,
changing planes at LAX.
Little Rock? Not my idea of wild.
Ruth has left a bad marriage, four kids at home.
Sally is newly wed, so happy she says,
yet still she's looking to hook up.
Dave, the married coat-and-tie to my left,
leans across me to work them.
He sells, sells, sells.
But mostly sells himself.

He has a heart, though, I can tell.
He lifts my bag, heavy with poetry,
puts them in the overhead,
makes sure I was settled.
I watch him put on a show for Ruth and Sally.
flexing his muscles, flexing everything.
He has no neck, seems kind, loves kids.

Some rogue scientist predicts doom for today, the 5th of May,
apocalyptic weather, earthquakes, volcanoes.
I close my eyes and see my children.
They wait for me on the earth below.
I see my young daughter straining at the ballet barre,
and my son, the four year-old hydraulic engineer,
building himself a carwash, complete with running water.

I imagine the cabin pressure dropping,
the plane plummeting,
and wonder if coat-and-tie-Dave would be a kind of hero,
maybe save my life, all our lives.
He's the type, I can tell.
But for now he is content to pick up nurses,
especially the happily married one with charcoal eyes.

The plane hits a bank of something.
Cloud, fog, air pockets, murk impenetrable.
The nose tips up, the flaps deploy.

How did I come to
this packed cabin,
struggling to breathe,
exiled from my children,
my Ireland,
my poetry,
my earth?

The Wide Net

It is an ancient and green land.
It is raining.
It is fierce.
Those who see the unseen are heeded.

I know things.
My voice carries to the far hills.
The people are hungry,
no words can fill them.
They chant hymns of woe, of war, of loss.

I have the gift of sight.
I look into the sea, the mother of us.
I watch the curraghs go out at break of day.
I know where the fish are.
I see where the fishermen must throw their nets.

I watch these men,
heavy with life, with rain, go forth.
I see the gold and silver fish, the life underwater.
Their nets are flung, woven from my hair,
yet in the dream they hold.

Then the nets rise, plentiful.
The fish feed my people, more than mere grass has done.
Sweet sounds of life are heard again.
Sad songs are remembered.

I wake.

Another Life

I recognize the hand
moving across my face,
a poet's.

So many years ago,
a man, in a savage place,
loved a woman.

I remember the insistent pull,
the shy sea-eyes,
my hair woven with leaves.

They lived a life.

I recall his voice,
a purr, a hum in the darkness,
the grave face.

There. Then.

I remember the fingers
seeking something
as if blind.

It was long ago.

Where have you been, he asks.

Here.

Now.

Always.

Stargazing 3:30am

In the middle of the night I wake and go
kiss my boy goodnight and cover him again.
His covers—his volcanoes, spaceships, caves—
have now deserted him.
I am his lone astronomer; I search his tiny face,
the fresh freckles, my vast night sky.
Across a Milky Way of skin, a play of stars.

Casseopeia flung across the bridge of his nose,
the golden head against the pillows, his Clouds of Magellan.
Orion Nebula acts as sentry on his forehead, guards his thoughts,
and Moons of Saturn ring the dusky eyes.
The Seven Sisters salt his peach-skin cheek,
and pale Aurorae stirs above a sliver moon, a brow.

These freckles are the only sign of her, his birth mother,
a girl who looms before me in the dark,
the body he was born from.
She must be waking now across the world.

Just where the ear is bent upon the pillow,
Andromeda bends to touch Pleiades, as I touch him.
And then, a flash, a new celestial fire,
a Supernovae, a thousand times brighter than all others,
his sleeping, dreaming smile.

Now That He Is Five

Each morning as his teacher bends
to guide his fingers into writing words,
her right hand supports her lower back.
Her belly moons and grows.
Soon she will give birth, as I did not.

Later, driving home,
from his blue booster seat in the third row,
"Sheri has a baby growing in her, Mom," he says.
He crinkles his nose, peppered with a new day's freckles,
rubs his painted cheek upon his sleeve.
"I didn't grow in your tummy."

We talk about Sheri's baby. We talk about him.
He knows his story. He has always known.
Hungary. Birth Mother. The American hospital.
The only photograph.
Even the music of her name:
Szilvia Sindular. Szilvia Sindular.

The world seems somewhere outside this car,
outside ourselves, my throat cuffed with emotion.
Through the rear-view mirror I see my boy,
the sweet strong body I did not make,
the golden strands of hair unlike my own,
the birth that did not pain me.

On the seat next to me,
a stack of the overdue library books
he cannot bear to part with:
volcanoes, tornadoes, glaciers,
tsunamis, hurricanes, earthquakes.
He can handle these.
He can handle this.

And then his voice pierces me again,
hoarse with allergy, heavy with asthma,
a remnant of the birthmother we may never see again.
He is quiet now, resolved. A slow smile curves
at the corner of his mouth like a flash of sudden sun.
"But I grew" he says, "in your heart."

The Little Warrior

I move my daughter's whitefish around on her plate,
searching for bones.
Her throat is so narrow, porcelain and pale.
And I have fears, where she has none.

As an infant she could not nurse.
No matter how I wished it, she could not draw the nipple in,
her mouth too small, her tongue not long nor strong enough.
She was lighter every day of that first month,
a baby bird fed with an eyedropper,
my milk dripping down her narrow throat.

"The Little Warrior" the doctors called her.
She had lived through months of siege.
When at last she unfolded at delivery,
long graceful limbs, finely-developed muscles yearning for space;
she did not curl up again, would not be swaddled
as the others in the nursery, tightly bound.
No. She gave herself over to life.

When I am satisfied the fish is bone-free, safe,
she rolls her eyes, what did I expect.
"You worry too much, Mommy."
The same coltish legs folded under her,
the same sweet mouth taking in food that will nourish her.

Now she is a dancer,
with grace and form rarely seen in eight year olds.
She switches position in the chair, sips from her iced tea, smiles.
Then she swallows, the whitefish glides down the same narrow throat.
The slender neck turns for a moment, away from me,
binding herself to a distant music.

ii

Purple Hyacinth

When the husband lost his sense of self,
the wife began to fix things:
a heavy wooden shutter, three chipped teacups,
the old Irish storyteller's lamp,
a slanting Venetian blind,
the missing grout along the inside of the tub,
a worn, beloved Hungarian doll.

Then there were the things to mend:
the son's sock, the daughter's ballet tights,
a brass button on the Aran fishing sweater,
one silk flower from a green velvet cloche,
a sagging hem on their daughter's uniform,
the slip that tore on their tenth anniversary,

Soon she noticed all the clocks were wrong,
and took them in for batteries:
the dainty wedding Waterford by the bed,
the boldfaced Parisian in the kitchen,
a jaunty harlequin in the children's room,
the cherry wood Georgian timepiece on the piano.
And still she lost all sense of time,
up so late she'd watch the day come in.

So she watered everything—twice,
tore dead leaves from the houseplants,
planted iris in the winter garden,
and filled the rooms with fruits and flowers.
The eggplant-colored den needed orchids
in a Chinese basket;
the scarlet walls of the dining room
called out for pomegranates.
In a carved Roman bowl she put branches
of forsythia with their promises.
Then the kitchen with a plate of lemons,
and by the hearth, a bunch of daffodils;
they had always made her happy.

For the children's room, blood red tulips,
in a heart-shaped vase for love of them.
By their marriage bed, an apple blossom,
for the Yeats poem she'd always loved.
And by the window, in the sunlight,
one purple hyacinth in a terracotta pot,
for hope.

Lifeboat

Once the marriage bed
was a lifeboat

where we clung,
alive and present,

in our bodies,
held in by skin,

as the waters rose around us,
and the tide drew us further out to sea.

a man is an island

he is an island
i visit in my mind
island of otherness
island of mystery

there breathes a holy happiness
we carve it out of stone
he is the keeper of the flame
i write the poems to live in

we are both young and old there
and time is not apace
just the vast sea to enclose us
night stars to crowd us with their fires

he is an island
i visit in my heart
island of oneness
island of clarity

and from that fair isle of rock and green
one pure place of peace
we hurt no living thing

Threat to Earth

The meteor that hit Russia
kept me awake, vigilant, for days.
The way it split into fireballs of destruction,
and laid waste each place of impact.
That asteroid that just missed Florida last week,
the size of a city block, kept me up all night.
Far too close for comfort.

After all,
an asteroid had nearly hit us ten years before,
just grazed our lives, the night he left the first time.
We felt the singe.
I gathered the children and the dog,
moved back into my childhood home,
my parents' arms, solid earth.
I soothed the burns, sold our dream house,
waited for his return.

When he returned to us,
I believed in the miracle,
thought the inevitable had been averted,
the tragic course shifted by a single degree,
our lives saved.

A decade passed.
But what I thought we had averted,
returned, came back into orbit.
The end of life as we knew it.

I took my children from the burning fields,
drove north to cooler, wetter land,
summoned the will to go on
from the very center of the earth,
rebuilt our lives.

As the universe presents,
so must we adapt,

adjust to a foreign body coming in.
We have no choice.
Only survive the wake of it somehow.

The End

How to bury the body of love?
The sun scorches.
The ground shifts beneath us.

The truth can almost kill you,
leaves you just enough will
to keep breathing, facing day.

Home

If I am ever
without a home,
without family, friends,
without walls,
without possessions,
I will take myself
to the edge of the sea,
and live there.

The hum and roar of tides will be my music.
Pure white foam—
souls of mermaids
who've died of unrequited love—
my sea sisters.

The harmonies of blues and greys,
browns and glistening gold,
will grace my eyes.
My strength, the constant horizon.

I'll comb my hair with a broken shell,
make garments of seaweed,
learn to fish and gather rain,
decorate my cove with abalone.

In the sand,
my footprints
will be my only mark
upon the earth,
proof that I had lived,
that I had been there.

Until moments later,
when swept back into the sea
by a great tide.

Grief

I sit on my mother's grave,
the ground damp after rain.
Grass overtakes the brass plaque,
almost silencing the dates of her birth and death.
I prune and trim, till all is perfect,
then place peonies, her favorite flower,
in the rusted water canister.

It is as if she has birthed me again,
but this time flung me into the world
without her.

I see her emerald eyes, her smile of such kindness,
long auburn waves, flawless skin,
She was often stopped on east coast trains,
and asked for her autograph as Maureen O'Hara.

I run my fingers through the grass,
wishing she could feel me there,
wishing I could feel her.

I say her name.
Roberta Faith Patterson Grady.
No one hears me.

Few around today,
just one large family down the hill
gathers with their dead.
A sprawling picnic—
tamales, drinks, mariachis—
celebrating life.
The music drifts up to me on the breeze.

I polish the brass plaque,
whisper her baby's name,
carved next to hers,
her three-day-old son, buried with her.

How will I celebrate her life,
go on without her,
with grief that binds and breaks?
Mother, gone. Brother, I did not know.

I sit for a time.
Then from the grass,
from the breeze,
from somewhere,
comes an answer:
flowers, food, rain, earth,
those we love,
music on the air.

Mother: Sense Memory

Half a yard of pale lavender,
a small worn undershirt,
which care instructions read:
Machine wash cold,
gentle cycle,
wash with like colors,
non-chlorine bleach,
tumble dry low.
But I do none of it.
It will never be washed,
or ironed or dried.
It will remain as is,
holding the holy scent of her last day,
last hours, last moments, her self.

I take it out of its hiding place;
there is a fine blue scalloped edging,
a Fra Angelico Madonna's veil blue.
How like her these colors, this softness.
I breathe her in.
I cover my chest, my heart,
breathe into this breastplate,
once that of a saint.
There is some solace here.
I smooth the wrinkles,
fold it, smooth it again.
so worn from the year of dying,
of constant washings.
Now it never will be washed again.

I slip it home, inside my childhood pillowcase,
press the fabric into place.
It seems light, airy, even when enclosed.
Skin could breathe in this,
yes, one could breathe in this.
If one did not have to stop breathing;
if one did not have to die.

Safe Home

Just before parting
the poet said something in Irish
about truth and the eyes of a cat.
But I could not hold it;
I could not remember.

Only felt the round weight of it,
the still, disguised arrow,
the stone upon which to build a new life.

"Safe home," the poet said.
The air brightened around us.
Take me with you, I did not say.
Home. Ireland. You.

That Which Shines

I lift water to my father's lips, tuck his Irish blanket round him,
fill his hospice room with Pavarotti's voice.
He has loved music, song, always.
Once choirboy, then pure tenor, now nearly deaf. *Gratia Plena.*

He was a man of power, law, academia,
of medicine, justice, and world affairs.
He now awaits the night's moon, the next nurse,
a diaper change, the visiting grandchild.

"It's great company for me," he says,
nodding toward the blazing fire.
At ninety-two, my father chooses his company well.
No more time for questions or many words.

As the outside world dims,
his inner world deepens.
And each day left, I look for what is most important,
shining from his deep blue eyes, now blind.

Something Sweet

My father never ate desserts,
avoided sweets, was sweet himself.

Now, at the end,
his daily chocolate protein drinks
replace his favorite Chivas.
A new kind of richness.

Once in a rare while,
he'll taste a solid food,
but only a bite,
a single bite of coconut cream pie.

I am glad such sweetness
will be his last taste of earth.

Hallowed Ground

There is a terrible beauty in burying the dead.
How the pile of earth at gravesite
has a power of its own,
the solemn file
of family first,
then friends,
the profound silence,
then the grate of the shovel against earth,
the physical strain of it,
the harrowing yet holy sound
of earth landing on coffin,
shovelful by shovelful,
saying you are loved,
saying you too are earth,
saying this is the last gift I can give you,
the one for which there will be no repayment.

Latcho Drum: Safe Journey

My teenage son suddenly says
"I don't know if I believe in God anymore, Mom."
I stare at his strong hand wrapped around
a glass of water on the table between us.
"It's just easier that way." High school was a struggle.
The way he says it, even more than the words, worries me.

It has been a long journey to this autumn day.
From Budapest, from birth mother, poverty,
from his Romany roots to us, this family,
this world, this time, this day, this moment.

He feels solitude bearing down on him,
seeks true friends, contemplates the big questions.
He is comfortable in music, Bach, cello and organ.
He writes poems, paints, creates, is often alone.

My golden boy tears paper,
words and phrases from the Tao Te Ching,
endless, the eternal, nothingness, the one.
and glues them to his canvas, mixes his oil paints,
a dark spectrum, and sweeps his brush into creation.
Planets, implosions, asteroids, shooting stars.
He is a mystic, sees what others cannot.
I see him wreathed in light.

When his adored grandfather dies that winter, eyes open,
meeting his maker, after a long life of goodness,
my son receives a parting gift from him, one most needed.
"Mom, I know that he saw God."

In the Romany language I want to bless him,
in all languages to hold him forever.
I remember a phrase learned in his homeland.
Latcho Drum, I say silently.
Safe journey to him. God be with him.

Shape-shifting

An apple is red and sweet
because it participates in the forms
of redness, of sweetness.

But what am I?
Woman, child,
crone, girl?

I say spirit.

I am formless:
air, ether,
incorporeal.

And if I bite the apple,
what am I?

Woman.

Amor Matris

She is there,
in the pale blossom,
the pouring of the tea,
the warmth of the water.

She lives in the eyes of strangers,
the humble answer,
the taking of my hand,
the yes.

She wakes me in the morning,
hovers, a hummingbird, by day,
turns the pages of my books,
braids my hair at night.

She sweetens the chocolate,
answers my prayers,
blows out the candles,
and dreams my dreams.

Shakespeare's Fingers

I dream of them,
quicksilver,
ink-stained,
the cuticles torn,
moving across parchment,
across time,
defining what it is to be human.

And my hands,
small, freckled,
those of an Irish potato picker,
write these few words,
trying to define him.

American Wake for Elizabeth Howick

On a steel grey evening,
the rain in waves against her,
my grandmother locked the door
of the Kerry schoolhouse
where she taught the farmers' children
and made her way to the sea.

Stories of an unrequited love,
someone named O'Connor she had lived for,
came down through family whispers.
She was only girl of eighteen,
leaving the schoolhouse,
her parents, four sisters,
and all she knew.

She crossed the country on foot,
rock, thistle, rain.
Eight days later she reached Queenstown
and boarded the *Campania* for New York.
It was the first day of spring.

I imagine her on the deck,
windswept, gaunt,
her eyes holding the last light
of green land
she would never see again,
her mind full of poems she knew by heart,
words shaped by stone, hills, faith, famine.

Ten days later at Ellis Island
she signed the manifest,
Lizzie Howick,
a new self for a new world,
and stepped into the April morning.

No word of her ever reached home.

She died too young,
widowed, penniless,
leaving two strong girls to grace the earth.

In the faded picture that remains,
her dark hair pulled back,
the eyes deep-set,
her thick brows,
the sharp cheekbones,
her lips a fierce straight line,
I see my mother and myself.
I see my daughter.

Spring

It is yet to be written.
And what is this?

The unseen, the unknown, the new.
The gossamer thread will catch somewhere.

O wild greening, dreaming, blooming, earth—
I may have found something, something true.

Throwing My Wedding Band into Irish Waters

At the moment the boat moved past the Delphi Valley,
where echoes of the famine cry out along the granite shore,
I heard my soul-self speak, *here, now,*
and slipped my wedding band from my finger.

I turned it once to read the initials, and the date,
then dropped the sacred golden ring,
symbol of the beloved, the eternal,
into Irish waters.

I have chosen this place,
the aperture of that valley,
the stone inlet, a molten emerald vale,
where they say more starved in 1847
than in any other place of pain.

The ring bobbed, at first,
the sea rough with wave and foam,
a flash, a gleam, current-carried,
then sank into oblivion.

There, at the moment of parting,
with rain cooling the searing pain of it,
water, wind, rock, and sky
were the only truths I knew.

This is a land where belief is all.
God. Nation. Church. Vow.
I had believed also.
My finger wore the imprint of half a lifetime,
a pale flesh ring where no sun had been.

Sometimes in my dreams,
I dive to find my wedding band.
I comb the silt, the sludge,
digging, clawing, frantic to find it,
lungs straining,

till at last I see a glint of gold
in the murky depths,
half-sunken in sand.
Despite the longing, despite the loss,
I do not pick it up again,
but rise to the sea's surface,
to the dappled light.
I rise to the living air.

II

Convex

Famine: Black '47

In the winter of that year
the Queen's landlords feasted as always.
And when they ventured out to inspect
their post-eviction properties,
they saw the blighted, black potato fields,
the dying and the dead.
They held fine French silk scarves
up to their faces to mask the stench.

Next to the road
in a ditch the dying lay,
raving with fever and puking yellow bile.
By the hawthorn tree
a woman, long dead,
her stomach distended,
pregnant with starvation.

Not far from her, two lovers,
their frozen bodies under a single shawl,
their mouths, teeth, tongues
stained green from grass,
the last thing left on earth to eat.

By summer,
only their bones were visible
in the fragrant bog,
stark and chalk-white,
pounded by rains,
howling in the wind,
gleaming in the thistle.

Bird Dialect

A female bird will find a mate
that sings the song her father sang.
Thus she learns him and lives him, again and again.
His stories woven through her in shards of sound,
decoding the facts of such brief being:
moisture, drought, longing, migration.

She sings his poems
onto leaves as she passes,
etching a mark for life.

Diamonds Were a Girl's Best Friend

There was a Hungarian girl
in Auschwitz who shat diamonds.
It went like this:
the last night in the Pest ghetto,
her mother sewed a fortune
into the hem of her daughter's dress,
to bargain for bread,
to trade for water,
to gamble for a hiding place,
to keep her daughter alive.

Days later, in the camp,
when first stripped,
the girl tore them out with her teeth,
hid them under her tongue.
And just before de-lousing
and full body inspection,
she swallowed them.

Next morning,
at the latrine,
she found them in her shit,
She had taken great care
not to sit directly over the hole,
but just to the side,
that her jewels would live.
She washed them with her spit,
rolled them in a pinch of dirt,
made mud to smooth the swallow,
then back into her mouth,
and through her starving body,
for safe-keeping.

For fifteen months
this happened,
just like German clockwork.
Each few days,

this way,
till liberation.

So now her daughters
have the diamonds,
soon her daughters' daughters will.
The Hungarian girl bought more than bread
with the love of her mother.
Courage.
Vengeance.
Proof.

The Creaking Door

Jane Austen depended
on the creaking door
in the hallway
outside her room.
It was her sentry, her guardian,
her ally in the war of words.
With the first creak,
warning of an intruder,
she'd whisk away her writing,
cover it with needlepoint or sewing.

There on the small round table,
next to the Georgian silver tea tray,
hidden from all,
beneath the woman's work,
a whole world pulsed,
and wit like daggers flew.

Motel Pool: Missoula, Montana

I lay out my towel, open my book, in the baking heat.
Dipping my foot in the water, I interrupt something:
two people in the pool, in the middle of the day,
middle of the summer, middle of America.
She cannot be his daughter. This must be some sad flag of middle age.
A man like this defying death could be poetic. But he is not.

They circle, two animals of prey in ritual flirtation, and not in fun.
She rises from underwater, slides up the front of his body,
kisses his navel like a lover in the dark, submerges again.
He never takes his eyes from her. She must be thirteen now,
bronzed and able body of a swimmer,
blind worship in her cornflower eyes.

He asks her next time would she like to bring her brothers, her sister.
"No, I want to be with you alone,"
the she-ray pouts, then holds her breath,
and swallows the length of the pool.

From where she waits, a high school Circe in bright blue chlorinated lair,
she calls out, "Dad, play with me."
He swims to her, grabs her left breast, laughing.
I gather my towel, my book.
I cannot swim. I can't cool in the wake of this.
I will abide my body's heat, that which I know and understand.

The Weight of Silence

Give Vermeer a window
and he gives you a world:

a bath of grey morning light,
the weight of silence in the room,

a blue velvet drape,
warm bread on the table,

and a single girl, half in shadow,
pouring fresh milk.

Shoes

Nina guards the shoes with her young life.
No one can take them, try them, touch them.

In Romania, Nina had soiled pajama bottoms,
sewn closed at the feet,
thick rough seams instead of socks and shoes.
Thirty minutes daily the children got to play,
sliding down highly polished hallways,
a brief respite outside their wobbly metal cribs,
closed at the top like cages.

So she longed for shoes.
Nurses, doctors, bureaucrats,
prospective parents,
she knew them all from the ankles down,
memorized how their shoes strode, stopped,
turned in upon themselves, marked the floor.
Shoes spoke to her.

The day Mary went to claim her,
after eighteen months of red tape,
war, revolution finally behind her,
Nina knew the walk, recognized the shoes coming,
the purpose in them,
saying *Mother.*

She watched the buckles click,
the gleam of the black leather, the rounded toe,
these she knew before she ever knew her first maternal gaze.

When Nina arrived in Los Angeles,
we brought her shoes in welcome:
leopard sandals, black dress-up heels,
purple patent leathers, pink satin ballet slippers,
white Mary Janes with diamond straps,
tennis shoes that lit up in the dark.

One mother greeted her with Ruby Slippers,
and that first year she would not take them off,
red glitter flaking as she ran,
leaving a shimmer where she'd been.

You had to ease them off her as she slept,
wash her feet and change her socks,
then put them on again before she'd wake,
or she would wail for hours.

And when she'd wake,
if her new family was sleeping,
she'd crawl into the closets of her parents,
her older brother,
take all their shoes back to her room,
hide them under her bed,
save them for the other orphans.

The Death of Emily Brontë

In the parlour of her father's parsonage she is dying.
Rejecting the local doctor's care,
the minister's blessing, her sisters' pleas,
any sustenance, her lungs filling with blood,
she wills herself to die.

She who sits with her back to the pulpit,
in her father's parish,
motherless genius,
was reared in a dank graveyard,
hewn in a wild workshop.

She is married to earth and crag, wind and fire,
scribbling myth into words,
and words into immortality.
Feverish, incapable of rest, blackening pages,
Emily is stricken by the lightning in her own mind.

9/11 Syndrome

The air traffic controller cannot rest.
Each day that he sees
a perfect,
cloudless,
blue blue sky,
untouched,
waiting,
perfect as death,
he thinks *September 11th blue.*

News of a Belfast Ceasefire

That day
on the Falls Road,
three pale children, just out for ice cream,
witnessed an ancient legend come alive.

The Irish children did not know
that a white buffalo
was a kind of prophecy.
After seven centuries,
a premonition of peace.

These children,
wielding the heavy hatred
of their fathers,
and their fathers before them,
knew home as barbed wire, rubber bullets,
and machine guns bearing down on them.

Ice cream cones dripping on asphalt,
the three saw the noble beast
force its way through The Peace Wall,
plastered with graffiti and pain,
the wall that divided them all.

Lieserl Einstein

Einstein had a daughter he never knew.
She was the wild card in his life,
not light, not every particle a promise,
each line a curve,
an order behind all,
not faith in nebula,
not these,
her.
He knew the rest.

She died young.
He had left her mother just before her birth,
wed himself to other mysteries,
cast his mind among the Magellanic clouds,
conjuring a face he could not see,
asking of life other questions—
of time and space,
why and how,
and whether God
would have things any other way.

Union Workers Speak From The Dead

The creased faces, the knotted brows were theirs,
long-lined with silt, grease, faith.
They had lived so that those who came after
would know one ounce less of hunger,
one notch more of justice.

They were not to reap the fruits of their sacrifice,
their bones cracked, broken;
the pick, the hook had severed limbs,
their homes burned out,
warm blood ran in the streets.

But their strength in numbers rose; they no longer stood alone.
Pure as agate, they were radiant in their fierce right.
Shining with their brothers, they were edged, looped in light.
Now they have a message from the grave:
Plant fruit trees where our ashes are.

Lockerbie, 1988

The local Scottish women
walked among the ruins
of the crash,
collecting scraps
of clothing in their baskets,
the residue of people
who had met their death there,
blown up,
shredded in the air.

These women gathered bits
of fabric from the site,
cotton, wool, silk and linen pieces,
took them to their houses,
where they washed and ironed them,
wrapped them in packets,
tied them with ribbons,
cared for them as best they could.

Later,
they gave a packet to each grieving family
who came in search of those they loved,
but found only clean, pressed and holy threads
singed along the edges.

Glass Pieces

Horowitz stopped playing
at the peak of his career,
convinced his fingers were made of glass.
Each time he struck an ivory key,
he feared a digit just might shatter,
the sound disperse,
and the shards of it recede
until there was no more.

Up Beech

for Jane Goodall

The place is Gombe. Kakombe. Home.
It is not imagined.
And she is its prophet, a strange white ape
in 1940's schoolgirl clothes,
drinking the amber light of Africa
in the grey sleet of a northern sea.

This fair girl climbs upward
in her English childhood garden.
She has a sense of tree, hears the sap rising,
despite the air raid sirens, bombings
that are the order of the day.

From her beloved beech,
with almost human limbs,
she sees the valley of the chimps,
conjures them.

No perfect roses, bench,
lawn and leaded windowpane for her.
No. This is her imagined throne of rock
and eternal time, rising from a myth of lake,
the sacred place she has yet to see.

From there she speaks to creatures teeming in her mind,
lion and silver dagaa, black rhino, dik-diks and gazelle,
converses with her brothers, sisters — chimps.

The girl flies outside her self, into the secret heart of life,
knows ways to teach the world to come, renounces all else.
God hands her heaven in those high beech branches.
She is thankful, answers in Chimp.

Ode to Robert Frost

Pure American tree,
his blood branches stunted,

three doomed children—
one a suicide, one insane,

one dead at birth,
the silent one.

While he was rooted
among the poems,

carving a country
out of air,

a thousand trees
he did not know he had,

feasting there among the dead,
the living.

Manicure/Pedicure at Celebrity Nail

Lien stoops over my feet, cutting back the cuticles, dabbing with the oil.
She is working with a zeal her mother would have had,
planting stalks of rice in water, knee high in mud,
in the village of Thang Duc,
a world away from where she works now at *Celebrity Nail*
$19 MANICURE/PEDICURE SPECIAL
NO APPOINTMENT NECESSARY
ALWAYS OPEN

Her blue black hair feathers against my leg as she buffs and shines.
I take my first slow breath of the day and look around me.
Seven daughters of Southeast Asia working hard,
with oranges for Buddha in the corner plastic shrine.

"Daughter?"
She always asks about my daughter,
she still remembers her from years ago,
her sixth birthday manicure, wanting every nail a different color.
She too is someone's daughter. I wonder was she orphaned.
Her strong hands massage my feet, my calves, with thick blue lotion
and I think about the napalm, Agent Orange, limbs in search of bodies.

"Color?"
This is the only other question she asks, the only other word.
I imagine the bloodshed of the past,
and consider various shades of red she offers.
This time I choose a green I never had before,
the color of a field in Vietnam,
something verdant, something alive.

She takes my hands and places them before a tiny fan for drying.
I feel the past, helicopter propellers bearing down on me,
turning pages of the fashion magazines,
hear fifty-caliber machine guns roaring.

As I go to pay her,
trying not to nick the polish against car keys,

my wedding ring, wallet zipper, the inside of the purse,
I wonder why one is not so careful with a life.

I hand her a twenty, another five for tip.
But I want to take her hands or wash her feet,
perfume them with the oil,
dry them with my hair.

Redemption

There's a lonesome air
in the west of Ireland
where a young girl jumped
from the high cliffs,
binding herself to death,
to the famished rock,
to a shroud of sea.

And falling there,
the fierce wind,
unrelenting,
lifted her up again,
bound her feet to land,
to life,
howling
not yet,
not here,
not in this way;
it is not your time.

Cable Stitches in Bosnia
*for Jane Olson**

She went among them
armed only with humanity,
the hollow, haunted women.
Deadened, raped, widowed by war,
lost.

Overcome, she sat down,
took out her knitting and worked,
knitting them to herself.
Flashing needles,
fashioning a thing of warmth,
her work was prayer.

Her fingers drew them in.
Awakening, they moved closer,
gathered round her,
recognizing something
of their former selves,
something good.
A match lit in the dark camp.

She gifted them that day.
She said with her hands
we are all women,
we can create,
and you are still alive.

*Jane Olson headed a Human Rights Watch delegation
which documented atrocities in Bosnia.*

Dawn Breaks Over the Sea of Galilee

Only birdcall heralds this day.
A white flock in perfect symmetry
crosses the brightening horizon.

Here a drop of pure peace,
deep still water,
a mirror for ourselves.

And there the Golan Heights,
etched in shades of palest blue,
merge with what seems possible.

What is this inland sea teaching,
born at the heart place
of this land?

It opens not to the world,
to vast waters, but to us.
Drink of living water,
you who are divided.

On the Death of Seamus Heaney

The wordsmith breathes
and fashions letters into gold,
carves thoughts out of air,
molds perfect form,
shifts our consciousness,
conjures what could not be dreamed of.

And with two faint words of final wisdom,
"Nolle timiri," he left us.
Do not be afraid, he consoled,
facing death with that last offering.
He went alone to the island he'd envisioned.
The digging had been done.

What words are there for loss of him,
words of such inner radiance,
words that only he could summon?

Cake

Nobody knew who she was,
this woman
in New York,
who sent chocolate cake
by the truckload
down to the docks
to greet ships full of children,
refugees, orphans, spectres of war.

These hallowed souls,
small skeletons from Eastern Europe,
the last of them,
the ones who had survived the Shoah,
the ghettos,
the camps,
the hell,
were gifted with
cake.

The first taste of America,
sweet and full of mystery,
lingered long in them.
One fat slice per child,
frosting for frail fingers
where no winter gloves had been.

Fields of Memory

Even on the last day of his life,
an old Irish man in the Bronx
could repeat the names of every field
from his childhood,
fields he had not seen in decades,
fields he would never see again.

He had carried his native landscape
with him always,
counting internally,
naming infernally,
each field,
in perfect order
all the way to the sea.

Looking out on the tenements,
he conjured green before his eyes,
whispered his dearest ones:
the field of the stone of the cats,
the field of the farmer's curse,
the field of the holy well.

Acknowledgements

Jack Grapes, John L'Heureux, Eavan Boland, Seamus Heaney, Sharon Olds, Lisa C. Krueger, Peggy Tunder, Bronwyn Clare Reed, Aidan Ajándék Reed, Jane Olson, Tom Reed, Gabrielle Kelly, Stafford Grady, Kira Cahill, Erin Dignam, Brendan Grady, Natanjah Driscoll, Red Hen Press, Juliane DeSal, Claire Harrison, Molly Taylor, Patricia Ryan, Clare Dunne, Monsignor Connolly, Ann Marie Lee, Fionnula Flanagan, BAMBAZ Press, and The Incomparable Thursday Night Editing Class: Jean Katz, Alice Hayward, Elaine Mintzer, Kathleen Goldman, Laurie Jefferson, Patricia L Scruggs, Janice Gerard, Erica Jordan, Ronna Dragon, and Kathleen Wilhoite.

Made in the USA
Charleston, SC
15 July 2015